Wordwatch

Wordwatch

A plain language guide to grammar, punctuation and writing well

Deborah Bennison

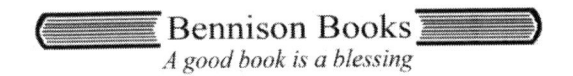

Bennison Books
A good book is a blessing

Copyright ©2014 Bennison Books
All rights reserved
First published 2014

With special thanks to Daisy Bennison

This book is sold subject to the condition that it shall not be reproduced in any form without the prior written permission of the authors and Bennison Books. Brief quotations may be used without permission in articles or reviews.

Cover by idrewdesign and fayefayedesigns

A Bennison Books Non-Fiction title
ISBN 978-1501017186

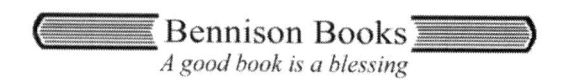

Bennison Books
A good book is a blessing

Contents

Introduction 1

Word Classes or Parts of Speech 3

Nouns 5

    Abstract nouns 5
    Collective nouns 6
    Collective nouns: singular or plural? 6
    Proper nouns 7
    Pronouns 7
    Different types of pronoun 8
    Personal pronouns 8
    Possessive pronouns 9
    Reflexive pronouns 9
    Demonstrative pronouns 9
    Interrogative pronouns 9
    Indefinite pronouns 10
    Relative pronouns 10

Adjectives 11

    Regular adjectives 11
    Irregular adjectives 12
    Non-gradable or ungradable adjectives 12
    Compound adjectives 13

Verbs 14

    Verbs: the infinitive 14
    Split infinitives 15

Adverbs 16

Determiners 17

    Possessive determiners 17

Conjunctions 18

Prepositions 19

Interjections 21

Idioms 21

What is a Sentence? 23

    What is a subject? 25
    Punctuating your sentence 26
    Starting sentences with And, But or Because 26

Active and Passive Sentences 27

The Subjunctive 33

Punctuation 37

Commas 39

    Using commas to separate items in a list 39
    The Oxford or serial comma 40
    Commas after introductory phrases 41
    Fused sentences or spliced commas 41
    Separating extra information in a sentence 43
    Defining and non-defining clauses 44
    Non-defining clauses 45
    Defining clauses 45

The Colon and Semicolon 47

    Colons and semicolons for lists 47
    When not to use a colon for lists 48
    Another important job for the colon 49
    The beautiful semicolon 50

The Possessive Apostrophe 53

    Possessive apostrophe and decades 54
    Possessive apostrophe: irregular plural nouns 54
    Possessive apostrophe and words ending in 's' 55

    The possessive apostrophe and time 56

Apostrophes Showing Omission 57

    Who's or whose? 57
    Your or you're? 58
    Is it its or it's? 59

Punctuation (When Using Brackets/Parentheses) ... 61

Speech Marks or Quotation Marks 63

    Breaking up your quotes 64
    Quotes within quotes 64
    Quotes that last several paragraphs 65
    Reported speech 66

Hyphens 68

    Hyphens to avoid confusion 68
    Hyphens and numbers 69
    Hyphens and points of the compass 70
    Hyphens and proper names 70
    Hyphens and the names of winds 71
    Using hyphens to separate identical letters 71
    Hyphens and 'un' words 72
    Hyphens and compound nouns 73
    Hyphens and compound adjectives 74

Commonly Confused and Just Plain Wrong 77

    That or Which? 79
    Fewer or Less? 81
    Affect or Effect? 83
    Amend or Emend? 85
    Lay and Lie 86
    Practice or Practise? 88
    A Hotel or an Hotel? 90
    My Friends and I or My Friends and Me? 91

Singular or Plural? 95
    Or 97
    Either 98
    Neither 98
    Each 98
    The number of 99
    A number of 99
    Fractions 99
    None 100

Double Negatives 101
    Correct use of the double negative 104

Politically Correct Writing 105
    Is a woman a man? 108
    Is a woman a girl? 108
    Gratuitous modifiers or the lady bus driver 109
    Jack of all trades: women in the workplace 110
    Ladies first? 111
    Their and them for his/hers and him/her 112
    Less of the ess 113
    Ageism 114
    Sexual preference or sexual orientation? 114
    Gender identity disorder? 114
    Physical and mental conditions 115
    Wheelchair users 116
    Handicapped 116
    Deaf and not so dumb 117
    Blindingly obvious 118
    Mentally handicapped 118
    Down's syndrome 119
    Mental health issues 119
    Defining autism 120

Accents, Dialects, Received Pronunciation and Standard English 121

    Accent 123
    Received pronunciation 123
    Dialect 124
    Standard English 124

Foreign Words and Phrases 125

    Foreign Words and Phrases: Index 158

About the Author 165

Bennison Books 166

Introduction

This is a basic guide to writing well. Aspects of grammar and punctuation that commonly cause confusion are demystified in plain English.

You'll find clear instructions on the correct use of possessive apostrophes, commas, speech marks, hyphens, and semicolons. Other topics include the subjunctive, split infinitives, and the difference between 'fewer' and 'less'.

You can also learn more about active and passive sentences (active sentences will often make your writing clearer and more direct); commonly used foreign words and phrases; and word classes, including nouns, adjectives and verbs.

Other common conundrums dealt with here include:

- that or which?
- affect or effect?
- lay or lie?
- practice or practise?
- whose or who's?
- my friends and I or my friends and me?

Why does correct punctuation and grammar matter?

Well, look at the following:

A woman without her man is nothing.

With the correct punctuation all becomes clear:

A woman: without her, man is nothing.

Wordwatch includes an introduction to politically correct writing. This is not comprehensive but offers some sensible, no-nonsense advice for the careful writer.

You'll find more information on the *Wordwatch* blog (wordwatchtowers.wordpress.com) where questions and queries about the use (and abuse!) of the English language are welcomed by the author.

Please note: *Wordwatch* is written from a UK perspective. Differences in American usage are noted where appropriate.

DB

Word Classes or Parts of Speech

Nouns

Nouns are words that name someone or something. For example, the following are all nouns:

carpenter (the name of a woodworker)
woman (the name of a female human)
table (the name of a piece of furniture)
guitar (the name of a musical instrument)

These nouns, and others like them, name people and things that we can touch and see. Nouns of this type are also called **concrete nouns**.

'Egg' is a noun. You can touch and see an egg, so the word 'egg' is a concrete noun.

Abstract nouns

Abstract nouns name things that we cannot touch or see, for example, the names given to emotions. The following words, which name emotions, are all abstract nouns:

love
hate
fear
anger

Time is another excellent example of an abstract noun.

We cannot see or touch time, but we know it's going by and we have to put a name to it!

Collective nouns

Collective nouns are names given to groups of people or animals. Examples include:

family
assembly
jury
crew
herd
flock
swarm

Collective nouns: singular or plural?

Most collective nouns can be treated as either singular or plural. For example:

The crew were very tired.

The crew was very tired.

If you're not sure whether to treat a collective noun as singular or plural, check in a dictionary.

Note that there can be differences between UK and American usage.

Proper nouns

A proper noun is the name of a particular person, thing, organisation or place. Proper nouns are always written with an initial capital letter or letters. For example:

Niagara Falls
Bobby Leach
Winston Churchill
Leeds Castle
Australia
Latimer Road
Cambridge University
World Trade Organisation

Proper nouns can be concrete (for example, 'Niagara Falls') or abstract (for example, 'Christianity').

Pronouns

We use pronouns all the time. They often help us to avoid boring repetition when we are writing and speaking. For example, look at the following sentence:

Shortly after John arrived, John decided to eat John's lunch and then feed John's cat.

Of course, we would really say:

Shortly after John arrived, he decided to eat his lunch and then feed his cat.

Instead of repeating the name 'John' we are using the pronouns 'he' and 'his'.

So a pronoun is simply a word used to replace another word.

Very often, a pronoun is used to replace a noun as in the sentence above where we see the noun 'John' being replaced with the pronouns 'he' and 'his'.

Different types of pronoun

There are different types of pronoun:

Personal pronouns

For example:

I
me
we
us
he
him
you
her
she
they
them

Possessive pronouns

For example:

mine
yours
ours
hers
his
theirs

Reflexive pronouns

For example:

ourselves
himself
herself
themselves

Demonstrative pronouns

For example:

this
those
that
these

Interrogative pronouns (used to ask questions)

For example:

who?

whose?
what?
which?

Indefinite pronouns

For example:

some
something
everyone
everything
someone
both
each
neither

Relative pronouns

For example:

who
whose
that
which

Adjectives

Adjectives are the words we use to describe something or someone.

For example, the following words in italics are adjectives (descriptive words):

the *beautiful* lady
the *long* lane
the *tall* tower
the *red* jacket

Regular adjectives

Regular adjectives can be used to show a difference in degree, for example:

beautiful, more beautiful, most beautiful

('more' and 'most' are called 'premodifiers')

Also, for example:

thin, thinner, thinnest

('er' and 'est' are called 'inflections')

Irregular adjectives

Irregular adjectives do not take premodifiers or inflections to show a difference in degree because the word itself changes instead. For example:

bad, worse, worst (We would not write 'badder' or 'baddest', or 'more bad' or 'most bad'.)

good, better, best (We would not write 'gooder' or 'goodest', or 'more good' or 'most good'.)

Non-gradable or ungradable adjectives

Some adjectives cannot show a difference in degree. For example, you can be 'dead', but you can't be 'deader'/'more dead' or 'deadest'/'most dead'.

This type of adjective is called 'non-gradable' or 'ungradable'. Other examples include:

complete
unique
equal
perfect

Some strict grammarians say that phrases such as 'very unique' or 'really unique' should not be used. However, 'unique' can also mean 'remarkable or unusual' and so it is OK to use such phrases, depending on the context.

Compound adjectives

A compound adjective is an adjective made up of two or more words.

Compound adjectives will usually take hyphens when they come *before* the person or thing being described. For example:

a high-risk strategy
a well-fed dog
an ill-equipped army
an up-to-date dictionary

However, if the compound adjective is used *after* the person or thing being described, the hyphen is usually dropped. For example:

The strategy is high risk.
The dog is well fed.
The army is ill equipped.
The dictionary is up to date.

And just one more thing…

Compound adjectives in which the first word of the compound ends in 'ly' (an adverb) don't take a hyphen. For example:

a poorly maintained building
a brightly coloured dress
a strongly built car
a richly decorated curtain
a badly cut suit

Verbs

Verbs are words that say what someone or something is doing or feeling or experiencing. For example, the following words in bold italics are all verbs:

The bees ***buzzed.***
The prime minister ***pleaded.***
I ***go*** to the shops every day.
Snow ***falls*** from the sky.
The table ***shook.***
She often ***speaks*** at conferences.
He ***climbs*** mountains in his spare time.
She ***thinks*** very deeply about things.
He ***expects*** too much.

Verbs: the infinitive

When talking or writing about a verb, the word 'to' is usually added. For example:

to run
to eat
to speak
to think
to consider

This is called 'the infinitive' because the verb does not apply to anything or anyone in particular.

You have probably heard the 'rule' that infinitives cannot be split. In fact, they can.

Split infinitives

'Splitting an infinitive' means to place a word or words (usually an adverb) between the word 'to' and the verb. For example:

to *humbly* beg
to *loudly* speak
to *thoughtfully* answer

A very famous example of a successful split infinitive is:

To boldly go where no one has gone before

If your split infinitive sounds better than not splitting it, split away!

Adverbs

Adverbs are words that give us extra information, very often about the way something is being done. We use adverbs all the time.

In the following sentences the adverbs are in bold:

She strutted **confidently** *along the catwalk and posed* **beautifully** *for the photographers.*

He groaned **quietly** *then* **violently** *pushed back his chair. The dog yawned* **sleepily**.

She spoke **thoughtfully** *then* **carefully** *wrote down all the questions that were asked.*

Adverbs are often formed by adding the letters 'ly' to an adjective (or describing word). For example:

- **confident** is an adjective: **confidently** is an adverb.
- **beautiful** is an adjective: **beautifully** is an adverb.

Determiners

Determiners are words used before nouns. These include:

a/ an
the
every
this
those
many

The word 'the' is also referred to as 'the definite article'.

The words 'a' and 'an' are also referred to as 'indefinite articles'.

Possessive determiners

Possessive determiners indicate who or what owns something. Examples of possessive determiners include:

my
our
your
theirs
hers
his
its

Conjunctions

Conjunctions are simply linking words. They make your writing smooth and easy to read; and can also help you add to the meaning of what you've written.

Commonly used conjunctions are 'and' and 'but'. For example:

*The cake is sweet **and** tasty.*

Here, the conjunction 'and' simply acts as a link word between 'sweet' and 'tasty'.

However, in the following example, the conjunction 'but' helps to add a second meaning:

*The cake is sweet **but** poisonous.*

Conjunctions also include:

or
yet
while
although
because
as
for
since
if

Prepositions

Prepositions are often used to describe where someone or something is or the time that something took place. In the following examples, the prepositions are in bold:

*The firework display will start **in** the evening.*

*The cat is **between** the fence and the wall.*

*The food is **on** the table.*

*I work **during** the day.*

Here's a list of common prepositions:

to
over
under
along
above
across
at
in
below
among
off
on
towards
with
during

before
after
for
between
beside

You've probably heard the mantra that you can't place a preposition at the end of a sentence. Well, you can if it sounds best that way. For example:

London is the city I'm going to.

Rather than:

London is the city to which I'm going.

And:

He's the person I'm going with.

Rather than:

He's the person with whom I'm going.

Trust your own judgement and place your prepositions where you think they sound best.

Interjections

Interjections are words or phrases used on their own. For example:

Oops!
Ouch!
Ah!
Oh dear!
Fantastic!
Damn!

These words and phrases are also 'exclamations' and so correctly take an exclamation mark.

Idioms

Idioms are words or phrases that have a particular meaning, even though the words themselves do not explain the meaning. For example:

*It's **raining cats and dogs**.* (It's pouring with rain.)

*The exam was **a piece of cake**.* (The exam was very easy.)

***Let sleeping dogs lie**.* (Don't do or say anything further.)

What is a Sentence?

What is a Sentence?

Most of the time, we can 'hear' whether or not we have written a 'proper' sentence because it makes sense and it sounds right.

The *Oxford Dictionary of English* says a sentence is:

A set of words that is complete in itself

So we can easily see that the following examples are not proper sentences:

the book on the bookshelf
the torrential rain
a very long discussion

A sentence must always include a verb and in most cases will also include a subject.

What is a subject?

The subject in a sentence is the person or thing that the sentence is about, or the person or thing doing something. Let's make the examples above into sentences.

We can change *the book on the bookshelf* to:

I put the book on the bookshelf.

We have added the subject 'I' and the verb 'put'.

We can change *the torrential rain* to:

They walked in the torrential rain.

We have added the subject 'they' and the verb 'walked'.

We can change *a very long discussion* to:

The ministers ended a very long discussion at midnight.

We have added the subject 'the ministers' and the verb 'ended'.

Punctuating your sentence

A sentence always starts with a capital letter and will end with a full stop, question mark or exclamation mark.

Starting sentences with And, But or Because

Can you start sentences with 'And'?

Yes.

And you can also start sentences with 'But' and 'Because'.

But don't do it too often. And avoid doing so indiscriminately. Because that would get boring.

Active and Passive Sentences

Active or Passive?

George Orwell, who was passionate about writing in plain language, wrote in his essay *Politics and the English Language* (1950):

Never use the passive where you can use the active.

How to recognise a passive sentence

Very often, you can recognise a passive sentence because you can't tell who is responsible for doing something. Here is a passive sentence:

You will be sent a letter within six weeks.

You know it's passive because you don't know **who** will be sending the letter.

Here are a few more passive sentences:

Payments will be taken from your account every month. (You don't know who will take the payments.)

Residents are visited if they have any complaints. (You don't know who will visit the residents.)

You will be telephoned when the outcome is known. (You don't know who will telephone.)

You can see that these sentences are a little long-winded, impersonal and slightly pompous. Some officials love the passive because it distances them from their readers; readers often have no way of knowing who will carry out the promised action and so no one can easily be called to account.

Active sentences

You can transform your sentences by making them active:

I will send you a letter within six weeks.

We will take payments from your account every month.

We visit residents if they have any complaints.

I will telephone you when I know the outcome.

If you want your writing to be clear and direct, the active will usually be a much better choice than the passive.

When the passive is friendlier

The passive can be a good choice if you don't want to sound aggressive. For example, look at these active sentences:

You have ignored my letters.

You did not settle your account.

You have made a mistake.

The passive will help you sound friendlier:

My letters have been ignored.

Your account has not been settled.

A mistake has been made.

When the passive is the only choice

In some cases, you will have to use the passive. For example, look at the following **active** sentence:

Mr Green marked my exam paper on Saturday.

But what if you don't know who marked the exam paper? You would have to write the following **passive** sentence:

My exam paper was marked on Saturday.

The passive: technical stuff

As well as the main verb, passive sentences usually have to include some form of the verb 'to be'. Forms of the verb 'to be' include:

is
are
was

were
being
am
will be

In addition, the main verb in a passive sentence has to change from the present to the past tense. As an example, look at the following active sentence:

I eat fish.

To make it passive, it becomes:

The fish are eaten by me.

The verb 'are' has been added and 'eat' (the main verb) has been changed to the past tense, 'eaten'.

The Subjunctive

The Subjunctive

The subjunctive form of the verb 'to be' (see below) is very useful because it allows us to imagine something that might happen or something we would like to be true.

The subjunctive of 'to be' is 'were'.

'Were' in this context is often used with the word 'if'. For example:

If only he were good at grammar.

If she were plumper, she would be beautiful.

If I were you, I would leave.

It can also be used without 'if'. For example:

Were I to go out I might see him.

And it can be used with 'wish'. For example:

He wished the day were over.

The verb 'to be'

The verb 'to be' usually takes familiar forms, such as:

I *am*

she/he *is*
you *are*
I *was*
she/he *was*
you *were* (this is not the subjunctive 'were': it is just the past tense. For example: *You were at home when I called earlier.*)

Punctuation

Commas

The comma multitasks (so it must be female) and is invaluable to ensure clarity in your writing. The following examples shows how vital correct use of the comma is:

Have you eaten Mum?

Have you eaten, Mum?

The second version makes it clear that no one can be accused of eating Mum!

Here is another example:

Jane's parents, the queen and the prime minister, were there.

Jane's parents, the queen, and the prime minister were there.

In the second example, thanks to the comma after 'queen', it is clear that Jane's parents are not the queen and prime minister. In the first example, with the comma after 'prime minister', it looks as if they are.

Using commas to separate items in a list

Use commas to separate items in a list. For example:

I had egg, beans, sausages, mushrooms and toast for breakfast.

Note that you do not need a comma before 'and' in sentences like this. (However, see more on this below.)

Here are some more examples:

We went to Italy, France, Germany, Spain and Portugal.

I need warm clothes, a map, a packed lunch and strong shoes.

I am going to buy books, wrapping paper, a pen, a newspaper and milk.

The comma is not suitable for more complex lists: you will need the semicolon (see page 44).

The Oxford or serial comma

Look at this sentence again:

Jane's parents, the queen, and the prime minister were there.

Commas used before 'and' in this way when writing a list are called Oxford or serial commas. Sometimes, as in this example, it's necessary to use an Oxford comma for clarity.

Otherwise, use of the Oxford comma is a matter of personal choice or house style. So both of the following can be correct:

I like fishing, smoking, driving, playing cards, and swimming.

I like fishing, smoking, driving, playing cards and swimming.

Commas after introductory phrases

Always use a comma to mark a pause after introductory words or phrases in a sentence, as in the following examples:

Nevertheless,
However,
Indeed,
Of course,
Naturally,
On the other hand,
In fact,
Therefore,
In addition,
Having said that,
Following on from that,

When using these words and phrases in the middle of a sentence, they should appear between commas. For example:

I think, nevertheless, that I will go to the meeting.

I noticed that Jane, on the other hand, was not keen at all.

You will, naturally, want to visit her.

Fused sentences or spliced commas

People often use a comma when a full stop is required.

Here's an opening line from a letter I received:

I am pleased to enclose your original policy document, you should keep this in a safe place.

See how that comma placed after 'document' is groaning under the strain of doing the work of a full stop?

Using a comma when a full stop is required results in what is known as a 'fused sentence', or in the US as a 'comma splice'. The sentence above requires a full stop or semicolon:

I am pleased to enclose your original policy document from Legal & General. You should keep this in a safe place.

Here are some more examples of fused sentences/comma splices:

I don't know whether to wear the red dress or the green suit, my problem is that the red dress isn't back from the dry cleaners yet.

You can see that the comma after 'green suit' simply isn't strong enough. The result is a long, amorphous sprawl of words. The comma 'fuses' the string of words together into a 'sentence', but only under protest. The comma needs to be a full stop or a semicolon:

I don't know whether to wear the red dress or the green suit. My problem is that the red dress isn't back from the dry cleaners yet.

I don't know whether to wear the red dress or the green suit; my problem is that the red dress isn't back from the dry cleaners yet.

Here are some more examples of fused sentences; you can see that the comma isn't strong enough to do the work being asked of it:

The removal men are arriving at about midday, we need to contact the electricity company to give them a final meter reading.

He came into the room smoking a cigarette, the butler hurried over with an ashtray.

We have now looked into the matter, our findings are that further work will be required over the next two weeks.

In all these examples, the comma should be replaced with a full stop or semicolon.

Using commas to separate extra information in a sentence

Commas should be used to separate extra information in a sentence. If you have used the commas correctly, your sentence would still make sense without the extra information.

In the following sentences, the extra information is in bold. Note how the commas separate the extra information from the rest of the sentence:

*She drove, **without wearing a seat belt**, as fast as she could.*

*The book, **which was very old**, was worth a lot of money.*

The film, **which received bad reviews***, was not seen by many people.*

The hotel, **which will close soon***, is near the sea.*

The meeting, **held after work***, went on for hours.*

The sheets, **freshly washed and ironed***, were put back on the bed.*

My friend, **who loves to eat out***, is coming to stay.*

You can see that all of these sentences would still make sense if the additional information (shown in bold) and the commas were taken out. See more on this below.

Defining and non-defining clauses

Look at this sentence:

The climbers, who were injured, were rescued.

You can see that this sentence would work just as well without the extra information about the climbers being injured:

The climbers were rescued.

However…

What if some of the climbers were uninjured and only the injured climbers were rescued? In this case, the sentence would have to read:

The climbers who were injured were rescued.

There are no commas and as a result, the sentence tells us that **only** the injured climbers were rescued.

Here's another example:

The fathers, who had children with them, were allowed in first.

The fathers who had children with them were allowed in first.

In the first sentence we are given extra information about the fathers (they had children with them).

In the second sentence we are told that **only** fathers with children were allowed in first.

The terminology

Non-defining clauses

Extra information provided between commas in a sentence is known as a '**non-defining clause**'. In the following sentence, the non-defining clause is in bold:

*The climbers, **who were injured,** were rescued.*

Defining clauses

In the following sentence, the defining clause is in bold:

*The climbers **who were injured** were rescued.*

We are told that **only** the injured climbers were rescued. In other words, the rescued climbers are **defined** as injured.

Summary

Extra information in a sentence is called a non-defining clause. Extra (or non-defining) information is always placed between commas.

Information that defines exactly who or what the sentence is about is called a defining clause. Defining information is not placed between commas.

The Colon and Semicolon

Colons and semicolons are very useful punctuation marks. If you want to write clearly and well, you need to know how to use them.

The semicolon will also help you add style and flair to your writing.

Colons and semicolons for lists

A sentence listing a number of different things will often need a colon and then several semicolons to ensure the meaning is clear. Here's an example:

We visited a number of places on our coach trip: Leeds, Yorkshire; Swindon, Wiltshire; London; the Isle of Wight; and Canterbury, Kent.

Imagine what a geographical nightmare that sentence would be if only commas were used:

We visited a number of places on our coach trip: Leeds, Yorkshire, Swindon, Wiltshire, London, the Isle of Wight, and Canterbury, Kent.

Similarly, the following sentence uses a colon and semicolons to ensure clarity:

When preparing to move house, I had numerous jobs to do: liaising with my solicitor, who was based in London; liaising with our buyers, who were often out of the country; and sorting out all our bills and other financial matters.

The colon/semicolon construction for lists is also excellent when you want to set things out as clearly as possible on a page. For example:

When you visit our office, please bring with you:
-your passport;
-your birth certificate;
-your driving licence;
-your certificates of qualification; and
-any other documents you think we will need.

Simple lists and the colon

Simple lists (see also page 36) will be clear enough with a colon followed by commas (not semicolons) to separate the various things listed:

Peter had studied many different subjects: architecture, medicine, law and history.

When not to use a colon for lists

1. You should **not** use a colon after the word 'including'. For example, the following sentence uses the colon **incorrectly**:

I have eaten several meals today, including: breakfast, lunch, dinner and supper.

This should be:

I have eaten several meals today, including breakfast, lunch, dinner and supper.

You can see that the word 'including' does the work of the colon and so the colon isn't needed.

2. You should **not** use a colon after any form of the verb 'to be' ('are', 'is', 'was', or 'were'). For example, the following sentences use the colon **incorrectly**:

The members of the Beatles were: John, Paul, Ringo and George.

The cake's ingredients are: eggs, flour, sugar and butter.

These should be:

The members of the Beatles were John, Paul, Ringo and George.

The cake's ingredients are eggs, flour, sugar and butter.

Another important job for the colon

Use a colon if you want the second part of your sentence to explain, illustrate, or elaborate on the first part of your sentence. For example:

There are 5,000 books in the library: half of them are damaged.

He is determined to overcome his greatest fear: public speaking.

The result was inevitable: nobody survived.

The colon can also be used to throw new light on what you have already said, sometimes in an unexpected or comical way. For example:

Life's a beach: wet, gritty and cold.

When using a colon in this way, the first part of your sentence will usually be able to stand alone and would still make sense if you deleted everything after the colon and replaced the colon with a full stop.

Just a quick note: there's no need to put a dash after the colon (:-). The colon is a tough beast and can stand alone.

The beautiful semicolon

You can use the semicolon to join two sentences together to make a far superior one. For example, read this perfect sentence from George Orwell's essay, *Shooting an Elephant* (1936):

And afterwards I was very glad that the coolie had been killed; it put me legally in the right and it gave me a sufficient pretext for shooting the elephant.

Imagine a full stop after 'killed': although not incorrect, it would have ruined the whole flow and impetus of the sentence. (killed it, in fact.)

Get semicolon savvy

Firstly, a semicolon should only be used in this way when the two halves of the sentence separated by the semicolon could each make a complete sentence in their own right if a full stop were used instead.

For example, the following sentences could each become two complete sentences if a full stop were used instead of a semicolon (although you can see they are much better with the semicolon):

The dress is exquisite; the shoes are divine.

We travelled for a long time; the road seemed to go on forever.

She is the most beautiful woman in the world; the cameras love her.

Secondly, make sure the two halves of your sentence are closely connected in subject matter with one thought logically leading you onto the next.

Summary

Use a semicolon when the second half of your sentence follows on and flows naturally from the first half. You don't want to stop the reader after the first half; you want to draw them on.

Think of it as a gentle crescendo, or two layers of the same cake: hard to prise apart and more satisfying when eaten together.

When <u>not</u> to use a semicolon

If your sentence uses a 'linking word' between its two halves, you must <u>not</u> use a semicolon. Linking words include:

and
but
or
nor
for
while
yet

For example, look at these sentences:

He is so ugly in real life, **yet** *the camera loves him.*

Mary is very keen to go, **but** *she cannot decide what to wear.*

Thanks to those little words 'yet' and 'but' a comma suffices and the semicolon is not required.

The Possessive Apostrophe

The possessive apostrophe is the little squiggle (') that shows someone or something belongs to someone or something else. The rules are simple:

If one dog owns a purple dog lead, the apostrophe comes **before** the s:

*The **dog's** lead is purple.*

If two or more dogs have purple leads, the apostrophe comes **after** the s:

*The **dogs'** leads are purple.*

If one family has a very big house, the apostrophe comes **before** the s:

*The **family's** house is very big.*

If two or more families have very big houses, the apostrophe comes **after** the s:

*The **families'** houses are very big.* (Note the plural spelling 'families', with the apostrophe still coming after the s.)

If one building has just had new windows fitted, the apostrophe comes **before** the s:

*The **building's** windows are new.*

If more than one building has had the work done, the apostrophe comes **after** the s:

*The **buildings'** windows are new.*

The possessive apostrophe and decades

When writing, for example, the 1980s, 1970s or 1960s, you should **not** place an apostrophe before the 's'.

The following are correct (all without an apostrophe):

Patti Smith lived in New York in the late 1960s and early 1970s.

The 1960s saw many changes in society.

Shirts with big collars were popular in the 1970s.

The possessive apostrophe and irregular plural nouns

'Children' is an example of an irregular plural noun (see page 5 for more on nouns). It is described as 'irregular' because, you don't stick an 's' on the end of 'child' when you want to talk about more than one child. Instead, you use a different word: children.

Other irregular plural nouns include:

women
men
mice
oxen

In all such cases, the possessive apostrophe is placed before the 's'. For example:

The children's meal was late.

The women's complaints were ignored.

The men's work was very hard.

The mice's home was blocked up.

The oxen's owner had disappeared.

The possessive apostrophe and words ending in 's'

Look at the following sentences:

*Prince **Charles'** organic garden is his pride and joy.*

*Prince **Charles's** organic garden is his pride and joy.*

***Mars'** atmosphere is hostile to humans*

***Mars's** atmosphere is hostile to humans*

Which versions are correct? Well, this is a bit of a tricky area as grammar books disagree. The different opinions include:

1. The "Prince Charles's" and "Mars's" construction with the second 's' is the only correct one.
2. Either construction is correct.
3. Add an extra 's' after the apostrophe only if you would naturally **say** the extra 's' when speaking.

So, this is a bit of a minefield. The best advice is to choose a style and stick with it. Don't mix and match in the same piece of writing.

Note that where an organisation has chosen to use an apostrophe in its name in a particular way, you should do the same. For example, St James's Hospital in Leeds is always spelt with a second 's' after the apostrophe in James's.

The possessive apostrophe and time

Use the possessive apostrophe when writing, for example:

I will be travelling in two weeks' time.

The egg will be boiled in one minute's time.

She has three years' experience in this profession.

Promote him when he has had one year's experience in the post.

Apostrophes Showing Omission

In words such as those listed below, the apostrophe is used to show that a letter (or letters) has been taken out:

that's (short for **that is**)
it's (short for **it is**)
what's (short for **what is** or **what has**)
can't (short for **cannot**)

Who's or whose?

Who's is short for **who is** or **who has**.
If you've written **who's** in your sentence, read it back to yourself as **who is** or **who has** to check that you've used it correctly. For example:

The man who's (who is) playing the violin is very famous.

Who's (who has) finished their homework?

Whose is used in sentences where **who's** (short for **who is** or **who has**) would not make sense, for example:

Whose hat is that?

You would not write:

Who's (who is/who has) hat is that?

And so **whose** is correct.

Similarly, look at the following correct sentences:

The man whose head fell off is feeling much better today.

Whose turn is it to go first?

Try reading **who is** or **who has** for **whose**. Neither works, and so **whose** is correct in both sentences.

Your or you're?

You're is the shortened form of **you are**.

However, you will often see **your** written instead of **you're** and sometimes vice versa. This is because they both sound the same when spoken.

For example, look at the following incorrect sentences:

*If **your** happy with the goods, we will send an invoice.*

*We'll let you know when **you're** room is ready.*

These should, of course, be:

*If **you're** (**you are**) happy with the goods, we will send an invoice.*

*We'll let you know when **your** room is ready.*

The way to check if you are using the correct word is

to read your sentence back to yourself:

If you have written **you're** read this in full as **you are**. If your sentence still makes sense, then **you're** is correct. If not, you need **your**.

If you have written **your** read this as **you are**. If your sentence makes sense with **you are**, then you should replace **your** with **you're**.

Is it its or it's?

Its is a possessive pronoun (see page 9). In other words, it's simply a word that tells us something belongs to something else.

For example:

*When the car goes by take **its** number.*

This tells us the number belongs to the car.

*As you get close to the house, you can see **its** windows need replacing.*

This tells us the windows belong to the house.

*The cat washed **its** face.*

This tells us the face belongs to the cat.

It's (with an apostrophe) is simply a shortened form of **it is** or **it has**.

For example:

It's *a lovely day. (**It is** a lovely day.)*

It's *gone the way of all things. (**It has** gone the way of all things.)*

If you have written **its** or **it's** read the sentence out loud. Say **its** if you have written **its** and **it is** (or **it has**) if you have written **it's**. Then you'll know if you've got it right or not.

Punctuation (When Using Brackets/Parentheses)

Parenthetical information (information in brackets) is usually unpunctuated. For example:

He will go to the private school (which is near his house) for the next three years.

or:

He will go to the private school (which is near his house).

But what if a complete sentence is placed in brackets? For example:

He will go to the private school (this was decided by his mother) for the next three years.

or:

He will go to the private school for the next three years (this was decided by his mother).

In both these examples, you'll note that the start of the parenthetical sentence 'this' is not capitalised and there is no full stop inside the bracket after the final word of the sentence 'mother'.

An alternative is to write two separate sentences, one of which is placed in brackets. In such cases, both sentences are punctuated; the bracketed sentence begins with a capital letter and ends with a full stop inside the second bracket. For example:

He will go to that school for the next three years. (This was decided by his mother.)

You can use an exclamation mark or question mark inside brackets if you wish. For example:

He's not going today (thank goodness!) but will be there next week.

I've been told that he's not going today (is that correct?) but will be there next week.

Finally, note that when a sentence includes information in brackets, the sentence should still make sense if the information in brackets were to be removed.

Speech Marks or Quotation Marks

There are a few different styles to choose between when using speech marks (or quotation marks).

In the following example, note that the comma comes <u>before</u> the second speech mark and there's a full stop after 'said':

'The train is coming,' she said.

Or this can be turned around with the use of a colon after 'said', as follows:

She said: 'The train is coming.'

Note that the full stop comes <u>before</u> the final speech mark.

In both cases, the actual quote begins with a capital letter.

You can also use a comma instead of a colon, for example:

She said, 'The train is coming.'

The examples above use single speech marks (' '). You can also use double speech marks (" ") if you wish. For example:

"The train is coming," she said.

She said: "The train is coming."

Don't mix and match between the two styles in your writing: be consistent.

Breaking up your quotes

You may wish to break up your quote into smaller chunks. For example, look at the following:

She said: 'The train is coming, but I might change my mind and go home instead.'

This could become:

'The train is coming,' she said, 'but I might change my mind and go home instead.'

Note the position of the commas and make sure you put the full stop **before** the final speech mark.

Also note that 'but' does not take a capital letter because it is not the start of a separate sentence.

Quotes within quotes

How are quotes within quotes punctuated?

Here is an example:

She said: 'When he said to me, "I love you", I nearly died laughing.'

You will see that single speech marks are used for the main quote and double speech marks for the quote within the quote.

If you prefer using double speech marks for the main quote, you will need to use single speech marks for quotes within quotes. For example:

She said: "When he said to me, 'I love you', I nearly died laughing."

In all cases, note carefully where the commas and full stops are placed.

The American way…

Please note: here's how Americans would usually punctuate this example:

*She said: "When he said to me, **'I love you,'** I nearly died laughing."*

You will see that the comma comes directly after 'you' and before the speech mark in US punctuation.

Quotes that last several paragraphs

If you are quoting a long speech you will need speech marks at the start of each paragraph. However, you will

not need a speech mark at the end of each separate paragraph, only at the end of the final paragraph. For example:

Mr Smith said: 'I'm just about getting into this grammar lark. I didn't do very well at school, but I think that was probably down to me. I can't really blame anyone else.

'Mind you, I don't think our English teacher was very good. And the headmaster didn't have much idea either. The school itself was in a pretty poor state. It's funny how the memories gradually come back.

'Actually, now I come to look back on it, I don't think it was my fault that I didn't do very well at school.'

Reported speech

Reported speech is used to explain what someone said without quoting their exact words.

Look at the following examples:

Mrs Brown said: 'I'm so happy for Jack and he deserves his success after all his tremendous hard work and effort. I'm so proud of him and everything he's achieved.'

This could be written in reported speech as:

Mrs Brown said she was very happy for Jack and that he deserved his success after working so hard.

Note that speech marks are **not** used in reported speech.

Hyphens

The hyphen is difficult to pin down because the way it is used is constantly changing. However, there are some general rules that can be followed, especially when you want to ensure clarity.

Hyphens to avoid confusion

Use a hyphen or hyphens between words if the meaning will be confusing without. Here are some examples:

Three year old children

Depending on the meaning intended, this should be either:

Three year-old children (three children who are all a year old)

or:

Three-year-old children (two or more children who are three years old)

A little used car

Depending on the meaning intended, this should be either:

A little-used car (a car that's not been used much)

or:

A little used-car (a small, second-hand car)

The author's 20 odd books

Unless the author is being insulted, this should be:

The author's 20-odd books (as in, 'approximately 20 books')

Man eating tiger

Unless the man is eating the tiger, this should be:

Man-eating tiger

Hyphens and numbers

When writing out numbers between 21 and 99, use a hyphen. For example:

twenty-one

eighty-nine

You don't need a hyphen when writing out numbers of 100 or higher, for example:

one hundred

five hundred

However, numbers such as 128 or 345 should be written:

one hundred and twenty-eight

three hundred and forty-five

Hyphens and points of the compass

Points of the compass should take a hyphen, for example:

north-east
north-easterly
south-west
south-westerly
south-by-south-east

Hyphens and proper names

Capitalise points of the compass when they are part of a place name, for example:

South-East Asia
North-West Passage

However, note exceptions which do not take a hyphen, such as:

Northwest Territories (territory of northern Canada)
Northwest Territory (now Indiana, Ohio, Michigan, Illinois and Wisconsin)

Hyphens and the names of winds

The names of winds are not hyphenated, for example:

northwester
southeaster

The American way

In the US, fewer hyphens are used. For example, the following are correct:

southeast
Southeast Asia

Using hyphens to separate identical letters

In the UK, some words are hyphenated to separate two identical letters. For example:

co-opt
coat-tails
pre-empt
pre-eminent

However, in the UK:

co-ordinate can be *coordinate*.
co-operate can be *cooperate*.

Choose which you prefer, but don't swap between the different versions in your writing.

Americans are much less fond of hyphens than the Brits, and all of the above words do not take a hyphen in US English, except 'co-opt'.

Note that some words do not take a hyphen to separate identical letters, for example:

override
overripe
overrun
overreach
overrule
underrate
withhold

Consistency and logic are not words that spring to mind when it comes to hyphens. There's only one answer if you're not sure: check in a dictionary. Sometimes, different dictionaries will give you different answers. In such cases, select which you prefer and be consistent.

Hyphens and 'un' words

The vast majority of 'un' words do not take a hyphen, for example:

unable
unaffected
uncaged
unarmed
unworried
uninviting
uncooperative

However, be wary of capitalised words such as *un-British* which do take a hyphen.

Hyphens and compound nouns

A compound noun (or 'noun compound' as the *Oxford Dictionary of English* has it) is a noun made up of two or more words. (See page 5 for more on nouns.) Should compound nouns be hyphenated?

Unfortunately, there are no clear-cut rules to follow, and in many cases a compound noun can be two words with a hyphen, two words without a hyphen, or two words run together. For example, all of the following are correct:

air-stream
air stream
airstream

Dictionaries may list only one option, but this does not necessarily mean that other versions of the compound noun are wrong. Here are a few examples:

boatman

greatcoat
cookhouse
anti-hero
fund-raiser
goody-goody
air pistol
high chair
hook nose

Compound nouns made up of three words will often take hyphens, for example:

man-of-war
sister-in-law (plural: *sisters-in-law*)
no-man's-land

But, as ever with hyphens, there is no hard and fast rule; 'prisoner of war', for example, is also correct with hyphens (prisoner-of-war).

Hyphens and compound adjectives

A compound adjective is an adjective made up of two or more words.

Compound adjectives will usually take hyphens when they come before the person or thing being described. For example:

a high-risk strategy
a well-fed dog
an ill-equipped army
an up-to-date dictionary

However, if the compound adjective is used <u>after</u> the person or thing being described, the hyphen is usually dropped. For example:

The strategy is high risk.
The dog is well fed.
The army is ill equipped.
The dictionary is up to date.

And just one more thing…

Compound adjectives in which the first word of the compound ends in 'ly' (an adverb) never take a hyphen. For example:

a poorly maintained building
a brightly coloured dress
a strongly built car
a richly decorated curtain
a badly cut suit

Commonly Confused and Just Plain Wrong

That or Which?

That defines and **which** informs (or tells us something).

For example:

This is the house that Jack built.

The house around the corner, which his brother built, is being demolished.

In the first sentence the word 'that' is used to distinguish the house that Jack built from any other house.

In the second sentence the word 'which' is used to provide some additional information. This additional information could be taken out and the rest of the sentence would still make sense:

The house around the corner is being demolished.

So, as a general rule use 'which' when you are providing some additional information for the reader. This will often be as part of a clause within commas (for example, 'which his brother built') and can be removed without harming the rest of the sentence.

For example:

This is the book that Dickens wrote.

But:

The book, which Dickens wrote, is now a classic.

However, in all but the most formal writing 'that' and 'which' seem to be used interchangeably without too much of a rumpus being caused. And you can usually tell if what you've written 'sounds' right or not. For example, you would never write:

The car which you crashed, that was the latest model, was almost brand new.

The correct version is, of course:

The car that you crashed, which was the latest model, was almost brand new.

Fewer or Less?

Fewer refers to separate items that can be counted. For example, items of shopping in a basket.

Less refers to bulk or quantity: stuff that can't be counted.

For example:

less shopping, fewer items

less bread, fewer slices

less concrete, fewer paving slabs

Segments or fractions

A segment, such as a half or a quarter, should be seen as a single quantity. Therefore, the following are correct (grammatically, that is, don't quote the statistics):

Less than a quarter of the population likes going to the opera.

Less than a third of the cake has been eaten.

Less than half of the town's pensioners live alone.

Money

When talking about money, amounts such as £50 should be seen as a single quantity, and therefore 'less than £50' is correct. For example:

The supermarket is offering customers the chance to talk to friends and family via their computers for an upfront cost of less than £20.

Measured amounts

A measured amount of something should be seen as a single quantity. For example:

The pool needs less than 30 gallons of water to top it up.

Time

When talking about time such as weeks, years or minutes, use 'less':

I'll be there in less than two hours.

It'll take no less than five years to complete.

Affect or Effect?

To **affect** means:

1. To influence or change, for example:

*Her hard work **affected** the outcome of the project.*
*The disease **affected** his appetite.*

2. To make someone feel an emotion, for example:

*Her speech **affected** him deeply.*
*The speech was very **affecting**.*

3. To pretend, for example:

*He **affected** to love her.*

4. To imitate or act in a pretentious way, for example:

*He **affected** a posh accent.*

To **effect** means:

1. To get something done or to achieve something, for example:

*He **effected** a change for the better.*

2. The outcome or result, for example:

*The **effect** of the speech was to change all our minds.*

3. To start to work or produce results, for example:

*The medicine began to take **effect**.*

4. A figure of speech meaning 'in fact' or 'practically speaking', for example:

*The decision will, in **effect**, be of little consequence.*

Amend or Emend?

Confusingly, these words are similar but not identical in meaning.

Emend means to make corrections and revisions to a text. For example:

*I will **emend** the introduction to my report.*

*The article has several spelling mistakes and needs to be **emended**.*

Amend can also mean to make minor changes to a text. But it is also used in other contexts. For example:

*The legislation needs to be **amended** to take account of changing circumstances.*

*I will **amend** the rule so it is fairer.*

*She should **amend** her dissolute lifestyle.*

*I feel guilty and will make **amends**.*

How to remember the difference:

Think of the letter 'e' in 'text': 'emend' starts with the letter 'e', and 'emend' relates only to text.

Lay and Lie

The confusion over the words 'lay' and 'lie' is widespread.

Lie means to recline, or to be in a prostrate position, or for something to be on a (usually horizontal) surface.

Lay means to put something down. This can be something tangible such as a carpet, or something intangible, such as the law:

I will lay the carpet and then I will lie on it.

After laying down the law she'll need a long lie down.

They will lie on the beach; he will lie in bed until he is better; the book lies on the table.

A hen lays an egg; the plumber lays his tools on the floor; gas companies lay pipes.

The past tense

Brace yourself.

Laid is the past tense of **lay**.

But:

Lay is the past tense of **lie**.

However, it's easier to remember than it looks: **lay** cannot be the past tense of **lay** so it must be the past tense of **lie**.

Summary

Here are the different ways the word **lie** can be used:

I lie on the beach.
I am lying on the beach.
I had lain on the beach for some hours before the sun went in.
I lay (past tense of lie) *on the beach for a long time and got burnt.*

And here are the different ways the word **lay** can be used.

I lay the books on the table.
I am laying the books on the table.
I had laid the books on the table by the time everyone arrived.
I laid the books on the table yesterday.

Practice or Practise?

In the UK, **practice** is a noun and **practise** is a verb. (See page 5 and 14.)

Practice

The noun **practice** is used as in the following examples:

The dental practice is within walking distance.
She has an accountancy practice in town.
I'll put my plans into practice.
The orchestra is out of practice.
Practice makes perfect.
It's good practice to look before you leap.

Practise

The verb **practise** is used as in the following examples:

She practises the violin every day.
The tribe practises cannibalism.
She practises dentistry (in her dental practice).

Practised

And if you are very skilled at something, you are **practised** at it. 'Practised' is an adjective (see page 11).

The American way

No such nonsense goes on in the States: practice is used as a noun and a verb, and 'practised' is spelt 'practiced'.

A Hotel or an Hotel?

Should we write **a hotel** or **an hotel**? Similarly:

A historical event or **an historical event**?

In the eighteenth and nineteenth centuries, the 'h' in words such as 'hotel' and 'historical' was often not pronounced. This pronunciation (omitting the 'h') can still be heard, and so it's still OK to write 'an hotel' or 'an historical event'.

However, the 'h' is usually pronounced in modern speech, and so 'a hotel' or 'a historical event' is just as acceptable. Don't mix and match between the two in your writing.

Of course, we write 'an honour' and 'an hour' as the 'h' is definitely not pronounced in these words.

My Friends and I or My Friends and Me?

Both of these can be correct.

There is an easy test to apply when deciding if you should use 'I' or 'me' in a sentence.

Look at these two sentences:

My father is taking **me and my friends** *out to dinner.*

My father is taking **my friends and I** *out to dinner.*

In this case, the first sentence is correct. The test is to shorten the sentences:

My father is taking **me** *out to dinner.*

My father is taking **I** *out to dinner.*

Now you can easily see that the first version is correct. You would not say:

My father is taking **I** *out to dinner.*

Therefore, you would not say:

My father is taking **my friends and I** *out to dinner.*

The correct version is:

My father is taking **me and my friends** *out to dinner.*

A similar test can be applied with the following two sentences:

My friends and I *are going out for dinner.*

Me and my friends *are going out for dinner.*

Just shorten the sentences:

I *am going out for dinner.*

Me *is going out for dinner.*

You can immediately see that the first version is correct:

I *am going out for dinner.*

Therefore, the following is correct:

My friends and I *are going out for dinner.*

Of course, when speaking or writing in a casual or informal style, it's not a hanging offence to break these rules!

Should I place myself last?

There are those who claim that the person writing/speaking should always place herself or himself last in the sentence. In fact, you can place 'I' or 'me' first or last; the choice is entirely yours. For example:

My father is taking **me and my friends** *out to dinner.*

My father is taking **my friends and me** *out to dinner.*

I and my friends *are going out for dinner.*

My friends and I *are going out for dinner.*

Singular or Plural?

Singular or Plural?

Should we write:

*Beef **or** pork **are** fine for the main course.*

or:

*Beef **or** pork **is** fine for the main course.*

A number of words and phrases present this problem, including:

or
either
neither
each
none
the number of
a number of
three fifths, two thirds etc

Or

Or is singular* which means it is correct to write:

*Beef **or** pork **is** fine for the main course.*

(*This means it is used with a singular verb. In this case **is** and <u>not</u> **are**.)

Either

Either is singular which means it is correct to write:

Either *the pot or the kettle **is** black.*

Neither

Neither is singular which means it is correct to write:

Neither *the pot nor the kettle **is** black.*

Either and neither: a slight complication

Look at this sentence:

Either *the pots or the kettles **are** black.*

Because 'pots' is plural and 'kettles' is plural this sentence is correct.

This slight complication is not too daunting, as you can easily 'hear' which is correct.

Each

Each is singular. For example:

Each *of the patients **was** seen separately.*

Not 'were seen separately'.

Each *of the reports* ***was*** *read in turn.*

Not 'were read in turn'.

The number of

The number of is singular. For example:

The number of *schools with good results* ***has*** *dropped.*

The number of *adults who cannot read* ***is*** *gradually falling.*

A number of

A number of is plural, for example:

A number of *schools* ***have*** *made improvements this year.*

A number of *adults* ***have*** *decided to give up smoking.*

Fractions

Look at these two **correct** sentences:

Three-fifths *of the people* ***are*** *happy to take part in the survey.*

Three-fifths *of the work* ***is*** *already done.*

The first is correct because 'people' is plural.

The second is correct because 'work' is singular.

You can usually trust your ears to tell you if the sentence is correct. For example, the following just sounds horrible:

Three-fifths *of the people **is** happy to take part in the survey.*

None

Is none singular or plural? Many reference works will tell you that it is definitely singular. But in reality it can be short for 'not one' or 'not any', depending on the sentence you are writing. So both of the following are correct:

*Of all the cakes on display, **none is** as nice as the one my mother baked.*

*Hundreds of boys were at the event but **none are** coming to the next one.*

Double Negatives

Double Negatives

Here are a few examples of double negatives:

I don't know nothing.

He doesn't want nothing.

They're not doing nothing for me.

She said she didn't have nothing to say.

It didn't come as no surprise to me.

Double negatives cause some people palpitations because, strictly speaking, they mean the exact opposite of what is intended. It's usually best to avoid them when writing and speaking formally.

However, using double negatives is not a treasonable offence. As the *Oxford Dictionary of English* (*ODE*) notes, the use of double negatives is widespread and 'rarely gives rise to confusion as to the intended meaning'.

The *ODE* also explains that double negatives are standard in some other languages such as Spanish, and were normal in Old English and Middle English.

Correct use of the double negative

A further interesting point is that double negatives can be used judiciously in all types of writing and speaking to add subtlety. Compare, for example, the following two statements:

I was not unimpressed with his performance.

I was impressed with his performance.

The first statement is, at face value, a simple double negative having the same meaning as the second statement. However, the effect is subtler: the first statement implies an all-important 'but…'. In other words, the speaker is politely communicating that they have reservations.

Am I Allowed to Say That?
Politically Correct Writing

Politically Correct Writing: A Brief Introduction

This is a tricky area. Many people get hot under the collar about politically correct language; they dismiss it as bonkers or some kind of threat from the thought police. Others – understandably – find the subject confusing (just exactly what am I allowed to say?) or are restricted to a house style that takes little account of modern sensibilities.

Having said all that, I believe it's important to do our best when writing or speaking to be inclusive and to avoid patronising and/or insulting people. This doesn't mean calling a manhole a personhole or studying herstory instead of history. The guidelines below will help to ensure that your writing avoids sexism, ageism, and a few other isms. As a bonus, the style and clarity of your writing should also improve.

The topics covered here include:

- Is a woman a man?
- Is a woman a girl?
- Gratuitous modifiers – or the lady bus driver
- Jack of all trades: women in the workplace
- Ladies first?
- Their and them for his/hers and him/her
- The 'ess' suffix
- Ageism
- Sexual preference or orientation?

- Gender identity disorder or dysmorphia?
- Physical and mental conditions

Is a woman a man?

Here are a few frequently used phrases:

the man in the street
the average man
the common man
early man
modern man
mankind
layman

Here are some sensible alternatives:

early man – ancient people, early humans
modern man – modern people or *human beings today*
mankind – people, humans, humanity, humankind or *the human race*
layman – layperson
the common man – the ordinary person
the average man – the average person
the man in the street – the person in the street

Is a woman a girl?

Is it OK to refer to a woman as a girl? No, not really. If you wouldn't refer to a grown man as a boy, why would you refer to a grown woman as a girl?

But when do girls become women? It can be a bit tricky, but just use common sense. Once you're in the territory of 18 years and above, 'woman' is always your best bet.

Otherwise, if that doesn't feel quite right in the circumstances, 'young woman' is fine, as is 'teenager' – although the latter is more suitable for younger teenagers.

I'm not saying that phrases such as 'a night out with the girls' or similar should be banned: that would be political correctness gone mad.

Gratuitous modifiers or the lady bus driver

A modifier is a noun used as an adjective. Modifiers become gratuitous when, for example, a bus driver is referred to as a lady bus driver because she happens to be a woman. ('Lady' is the noun being used as an adjective.) Ever heard of a gentleman bus driver? Similarly, we read about male nurses and male midwives, but rarely female nurses or female midwives.

Usually, it's women who have these gratuitous modifiers thrust upon them and the effect is to undermine, never to suggest superiority, as can be the case with the gratuitous modifier 'male'. A prime example of this is 'woman doctor', which makes for an interesting comparison with 'male nurse'.

Say goodbye to the gratuitous modifier. If I want to be flown to Paris, I want someone qualified in the cockpit.

In other words, a pilot. Or a pilot who happens to be a woman, no need to mention the fact, thanks for asking. But a lady pilot? Hmm, I'm not so sure. Didn't she miss that last pilot's exam because she had an important hair appointment?

Jack of all trades: women in the workplace

A number of job titles are male-specific. Fireman and policeman are prime examples, often used unthinkingly. The alternatives are more accurate and sound absolutely fine too:

firefighters
fire officers
police officers
the police

'Foreman' is OK if you are sure the person is male, 'forewoman' if she is female, or otherwise, 'supervisor' is a good alternative.

Similarly, 'chairman' is OK if you are sure the person is male. 'Chairwoman' is fine if you are sure she is female. Otherwise, options include 'chair' or 'chairperson'. Remember that some chairwomen prefer the title 'chairman' – respect their wishes.

It's always best to ask the person concerned which title they prefer.

Instead of 'businessmen', use 'business people' (unless you're certain they're all men, of course).

Women-exclusive terms can proliferate when writing about the workplace, for example, 'manning the phones' and 'man-hours'. There are many alternatives to 'manning' such as 'staffing', 'running' and 'operating'. Similarly, 'man-hours' can become 'work-hours' or 'staff-hours'.

Try to avoid popular but exclusive phrases such as 'our boys in blue' (a UK reference to the police).

Ladies first?

The convention of placing males before females when referring to people of both sexes is second nature to most of us. 'Husband and wife', 'his and hers', 'men and women', 'boys and girls', and 'male and female' are all phrases we use unthinkingly.

When writing about married couples, it's almost always the man who is named first, and when writing about a married couple's joint business (or indeed, a woman and man's joint business), it is almost invariably the man who is named first. Similarly, 'husband and wife team' is a commonplace expression, automatically churned out from many a keyboard.

The phrase 'man and wife' is an interesting one, the former being a person in his own right and the latter a 'married woman considered in relation to her husband' (*Oxford Dictionaries* definition).

Why not mix it up a little? Women don't always have to be mentioned first, but sometimes would be nice.

Their and them for his/hers and him/her

There is no need to write **he**, **him** or **his** when the **he**, **him** or **his** might be a **she**, **her** or **hers**.

Some writers who are doing their best to be inclusive use terms such as **s/he, he/she**, or **he or she** (usually in the traditional male first, female second order). While there is nothing wrong with this, it can be distracting to read.

The solution is both simple and grammatically correct. **They**, **them** and **their/theirs** can be used to refer to a single person who might be female or male. After all, Shakespeare wrote: *God send everyone their heart's desire*, and various dictionaries, including the *Oxford English Dictionary*, say quite clearly that **they** (or **them** or **their**) can be used to mean **he or she**.

So, the sentences below are correct. The underlined words refer to a single person who might be female or male:

Anyone can take their umbrella if they wish.

No one said their recipe was the best.

He heard them enter the house.

If they would like to take the exam we will ensure a room is ready for them.

Someone saw their dreams come true today.

Bear in mind that many people dislike the use of **their**, **them**, or **they** to refer to a single person and there is often an alternative way of dealing with this problem. For example, look at the following sentence:

It is the parent who should ensure his children are safe.

This could become:

It is the parents who should ensure their children are safe.

Less of the ess

You can safely discard the suffix 'ess' in most cases. Avoid, for example, words such as 'authoress' or 'poetess'.

Some '-ess' words are considered more acceptable than others: actress, for example, has a certain ring to it, redolent of Hollywood glamour.

If you are writing about a woman who wants to have 'ess' added to the name of her profession, abide by her wishes.

It is obviously still OK to use the suffix 'ess' when writing about female animals, for example, lioness and tigress.

Ageism

People of a certain age always seem to become 'feisty' or 'game' or 'spritely' or 'dapper' or 'lively' or 'nimble' or 'alert' or 'bright as a button'.

Drop the clichés. If you wouldn't use these words to describe a younger person, avoid using them to describe an older one.

I'm avoiding the phrase 'old people'. I know it shouldn't, but it sounds pejorative (probably because of our youth-obsessed culture), as does 'the elderly'. Prefer 'older people'.

Avoid describing an incidence of confusion or forgetfulness as a 'senior moment'. People can find this offensive.

Sexual preference or sexual orientation?

Avoid the term 'sexual preference' as this suggests some kind of lifestyle choice. Prefer the term 'sexual orientation'.

Gender identity disorder?

In 2012, the *Diagnostic and Statistical Manual (DSM) of Mental Disorders*, an influential American publication, stated that the term 'gender identity disorder' for children and adults who strongly believe they were born the wrong gender is being replaced with **gender**

dysphoria to remove the stigma attached to the word 'disorder'.

Physical and mental conditions

Describing people who have physical and mental conditions can be very tricky. But there are two golden rules that will help you no end:

Firstly, don't mention a person's physical or mental condition unless it's relevant to do so.

Secondly, don't hesitate to ask people how they prefer to be described (if any description is necessary: see the first golden rule above). If they cannot speak for themselves, ask their parent, personal assistant, carer or the person closest to them. Don't be shy about doing this. It shows respect for their feelings and preferences and they will prefer being asked to later reading a description that they will find patronising, insulting or inaccurate.

Here are a few more guidelines:

Avoid using general phrases to lump people together as a homogenous group defined solely by a particular condition. For example, terms such as 'the deaf', 'the blind', and 'the disabled' should be avoided. Anyone with a particular condition should not be defined as that condition. Never write, for example:

He's an epileptic.

No he isn't. He has epilepsy.

Avoid phrases such as 'victim of', 'suffering from', or 'afflicted with'.

Avoid calling disabled people 'brave' or 'special' unless you would have described them in this way if they had not been disabled. Being described as 'brave' or 'special' because you use a wheelchair, or are deaf or blind, is both patronising and a cliché.

Be aware that 'carer' can be a tricky word; the term 'personal assistant' or 'enabler' is often now preferred. Also, some people may object to this label (and that of 'enabler' or 'personal assistant') when they are first a parent, husband, wife, friend, sister, brother, son or daughter.

Wheelchair users

It's probably best to avoid terms such as 'in a wheelchair' or 'wheelchair-bound'. Phrases such as 'wheelchair user' and 'she uses a wheelchair' are neutral and respectful.

Handicapped

It is true that some physically disabled people don't mind how they are described, and have no objection to words such as 'handicapped', for example. However, others object very strongly to such terms, and it's advisable to avoid them.

If someone prefers to be described as 'handicapped', make this clear in your text. For example: 'Mrs Smith, who describes herself as handicapped'.

By doing this, you are showing your respect for the wishes of the person concerned, as well as your awareness of and respect for the views of those readers who object strongly to such terms.

Deaf and not so dumb

Unbelievably, the phrase 'deaf and dumb' still appears in newspapers and magazines, and is still used by broadcasters. It's insulting and inaccurate. The terms 'stone deaf', 'deaf-mute' and 'mute' are also best consigned to the dustbin.

Use 'deaf' or 'hearing impaired'. 'Hearing impaired' can be a good bet if you are talking about a number of people, as levels of hearing can vary widely from person to person.

If a deaf or hearing impaired person does not speak, be aware that they may be a sign language user (they are not 'deaf and dumb', or a 'deaf mute'). Don't refer to sign language as 'deaf and dumb language'.

Don't assume that people who are deaf, hearing impaired or members of the Deaf Community can be described as 'disabled'. People who are deaf or hearing impaired can deeply resent this description (as can those with other physical or mental conditions).

Remember the golden rule: if in doubt about how to describe someone, ask them.

Blindingly obvious

Phrases such as 'blind people', 'people who are blind', 'partially sighted', 'sight impaired' and 'people with a visual impairment' are all acceptable.

When referring to blind and visually impaired people generally, prefer the term 'visually impaired' as not everyone with a visual impairment is completely blind.

Mentally handicapped

'Mentally handicapped' is now an outdated term and in many quarters no longer acceptable. Nonetheless, it's important to note that some people believe the terms 'mentally handicapped' and 'severely mentally handicapped' are not only acceptable, but preferable to other phrases such as 'learning disability' which they see as denying the reality of some people's lives.

Remember the golden rule: if in doubt about how to describe someone, ask the person concerned, or if this is impossible, those closest to them. And remember: always ask yourself if it's necessary to mention the person's condition at all.

If someone insists that they or someone they care for should be referred to as 'mentally handicapped', make this clear in your text. For example: 'Mr Brown, who describes himself as mentally handicapped'.

By doing this, you are showing your respect for the wishes of the person concerned, as well as your awareness of and respect for the views of those readers who object strongly to such terms.

Down's syndrome

Avoid phrases such as 'Down's baby'; prefer: 'a baby who has Down's syndrome'. The term 'Down syndrome' is also used in the US.

Mental health issues

Don't confuse mental health issues with learning difficulty/disability issues.

As a general rule, put the person first when writing. For example:

Michael has a mental illness.

Anne has a mental health problem.

They have mental health difficulties.

George has experienced mental/emotional distress.

Avoid phrases such as 'Mary is mentally ill', or 'Paul suffers from a mental illness'.

Avoid using any clinical terms for particular mental health conditions (especially those frequently bandied about such as 'psychopathic' and 'psychotic') unless you are absolutely sure you are using the correct one.

Don't use the word 'schizophrenic' to describe anyone or anything unless you are writing about someone who has the specific and diagnosed condition of schizophrenia. Casual references to 'schizophrenic' opinions, attitudes or behaviour should be avoided. This is because the word is frequently and inaccurately used to describe a type of 'Jekyll and Hyde' behaviour, and perpetuates a negative and fear-inducing image of people who live with this condition.

Never say someone is in a 'mental home': they are in hospital.

Defining autism

According to the National Health Service in the UK, autism is defined as a serious and lifelong developmental disability. On its own, autism is not a learning disability or a mental health problem.

People with autism usually have difficulties with:
- social communication
- social interaction
- social imagination

However, some people with autism also have a learning disability, learning difficulty or mental health problem.

Accents, Dialects, Received Pronunciation and Standard English

Accents, Dialects, Received Pronunciation and Standard English

Sometimes the terms 'accent' and 'dialect' are confused, as are 'received pronunciation' and 'standard English'.

Accent

Accent refers to the different ways in which words are pronounced. Very often, the term 'regional accent' is used in the UK to refer to the way people from a particular geographical area pronounce words. For example, we have Scottish, Welsh and Irish accents, as well as those associated with cities such as London (the famous Cockney accent), Liverpool, Birmingham and Newcastle.

Received pronunciation

In the UK, 'received pronunciation' is an accent associated with the educated upper classes or 'posh' people. It is not possible to tell from received pronunciation which part of the country the speaker is from. The BBC now uses announcers and newsreaders with a wide variety of accents, but in the past only speakers with received pronunciation were heard over the airways.

Dialect

Dialect refers to the vocabulary and grammar that people use. An accent can also contribute to a particular dialect.

Standard English

In the UK, 'standard English' is a dialect. Standard English is considered to be formally correct. It can be spoken in a regional accent.

Foreign Words and Phrases

Foreign Words and Phrases

This is not an exhaustive or comprehensive list but it does include words that often crop up and are useful to know. It's best to use them sparingly as your readers might not know their meaning and dropping in foreign words and phrases can smack of showing off. Very often, a plain English word or phrase will be your best choice. George Orwell, in his essay *Politics and the English Language* (1950), has the best advice:

Never use a foreign phrase, a scientific word, or a jargon word if you can think of an everyday English equivalent.

He adds that the rule should be broken only to avoid saying anything that is 'outright barbarous'.

Latin words and phrases

ab initio

This means 'from the start'. For example:

The project was a guaranteed success ab initio.

ad hoc

This means 'to this/for this' and is used to mean 'for a particular purpose only'. For example:

Let's set up an ad hoc meeting to discuss absenteeism.

ad hominem

This means 'against the man'. An ad hominem argument is one where someone tries to undermine a proposition by making a personal attack on the person who has put it forward, rather than addressing the issue itself.

ad infinitum

This means 'endlessly'. For example:

The advert will run ad infinitum on the television.

a fortiori

Broadly speaking, this means 'for a similar but even more convincing reason' or 'even more so'. For example:

All the reasons given for expelling the head boy applied a fortiori to his deputy.

ad nauseam

This means 'to the point of nausea' and means going on and on in an extremely boring or intolerable way. For example:

He droned on and on ad nauseam.

alumna/alumnus/alumni

This means 'nursling' from 'alere' meaning 'to nourish'. These words are now used to refer to school, college or university graduates. Alumna being female, alumnus being male, and the plural alumni being used to refer to either sex.

annus mirabilis

This means 'a remarkable year' and can refer to a year that is remarkable or notable. For example, a year in which something catastrophic happened or one in which something wonderful happened.

annus horribilis

This means 'a terrible year'. Queen Elizabeth II coined this phrase basing it on 'annus mirabilis'.

ante bellum

This means 'before the war' and has become 'antebellum' in the English language meaning 'pre-war'. For example:

In the antebellum south, traditional ways of life continued unhindered.

Note that 'antebellum' is most frequently used when referring to the American Civil War. See also 'casus belli'.

bona fide

This is widely used and means 'in good faith' or 'real and genuine'. For example:

The pot is a bona fide relic from the Roman era.

bona fides

If you produce your bona fides you are proving that you are trustworthy and have honourable intentions. See also 'mala fide'.

carpe diem

This means 'seize the day' and is used to mean 'enjoy the present without worrying about the future'.

casus belli

This means 'justification for war'. This example is from a newspaper article:

Mr Blair says it complies exactly with his argument that the casus belli was Saddam's refusal to follow UN resolutions.

caveat emptor

This means 'let the buyer beware' and is used in situations where buyers should be cautious as they, not the seller, are taking the risk in buying.

circa

This means 'about', for example:

He was born circa 1920.

This can be abbreviated to 'c.' or 'ca.'.

cogito ergo sum

This is the philosopher Descartes' famous assertion and means 'I think therefore I exist'.

compos mentis

This means 'in full possession of mental powers' and is used to describe someone who is of sound mind. Its opposite is 'non compos mentis'.

cui bono?

This means 'who stands to gain?'. For example:

The law has been passed, but cui bono?

cum laude

This means 'with praise' and is most commonly used in connection with American university degrees as follows:

- Top degree: summa cum laude (with greatest praise/with the highest distinction)

- Second highest degree: magna cum laude (with great praise/with great distinction)
- Third highest degree: cum laude (with praise/with distinction)

de facto

This means 'from the fact' and is used to mean that something is in fact true whether or not the circumstances are officially or legally recognised. For example:

The unelected military leader is now the country's de facto president.

de jure

This means 'sanctioned by law'.

de profundis

This means 'out of the depths' and is used to mean 'out of the depths of despair'. *De Profundis* is the name given to the 50,000-word letter Oscar Wilde wrote from Reading Gaol to his lover, Lord Alfred Douglas.

deus ex machina

This means 'a god out of a machine'. It is derived from ancient Greek theatre when the denouement of a play involved a 'god' descending onto the stage with the help of a mechanical device. The role of the god was to tie up all the loose ends and sort everything out satisfactorily.

The phrase is now used to describe any completely unexpected event that results in a positive outcome. It is often used to refer to an extremely unlikely plot development in a creaky book or film (for example, the murderer dying of a heart attack just as he is about to plunge in the knife).

emeritus/emerita

This title is conferred on individuals who have retired from a full-time academic position but retain their title on an honorary basis. The first refers to a male, the second to a female.

erratum

This means 'error' and is used by publishers as a posh way of flagging up the fact that there is a mistake in their publication. 'Errata' is the plural.

ergo

This means 'therefore'. For example:

The man is dead and ergo cannot be punished.

et al (1)

This is an abbreviation for 'et alibi' meaning 'and elsewhere'.

et al (2)

This is an abbreviation for:

- et alii: 'and other men'
- et aliae: 'and other women'
- et alia: 'and other things'

et tu, Brute?

This means 'you also, Brutus?' and are the words attributed to Caesar when he realised his trusted friend had joined others in murdering him. Now the phrase is used to suggest any situation where a betrayal has occurred. It is Shakespearian Latin, rather than 'correct' Latin.

ex cathedra

This means 'from the chair' and is used to show that a person speaks with knowledge and authority. For example:

Her position as education secretary means she can speak ex cathedra on the subject of parental choice.

exempli gratia

This means 'for instance' or 'for example' and is commonly shortened to 'e.g.' or 'eg'. Some writers use this phrase incorrectly to mean 'that is'. See also 'ex gratia' and 'id est'.

ex gratia

This means 'out of kindness' and refers to something that is given as a favour or where nothing is expected in return. For example, an 'ex gratia payment'.

habeas corpus

This means 'you may have the body' and is the legal writ that underpins the sanctity of personal liberty under the British legal system. It means that an individual must be either freed or brought before a court of law.

ibid (scholarly)

This is a shortened form of 'ibidem', meaning 'in the same place'. It is used to refer to an identical source previously mentioned.

id est

This means 'that is' and is commonly shortened to 'i.e.'. For example:

I'm a vegetarian, i.e. I don't eat meat.

in flagrante delicto

This means 'while the crime is blazing' and refers to being caught red-handed in the middle of committing a crime. For example:

The police arrested him in flagrante delicto.

infra dig

This is short for 'infra dignitatem' and means 'beneath one's dignity' or 'undignified'. For example:

She thought doing household chores was infra dig.

in loco parentis

This means 'in the place of a parent' and is commonly used to refer to anyone who is looking after a child in place of the child's parents. For example:

She is acting in loco parentis while the parents are away.

in medias res

This means 'into the midst of things' and is most commonly used when writing about books that start in the middle of the action, as in this example from a newspaper article:

In medias res is how most of the novels begin, with children hurried into a story that has already begun.

inter alia

This means 'among other things'. For example:

The food and service, inter alia, has completely put me off the hotel.

See also 'inter alios'.

inter alios

This means, 'among other people'. For example:

She works for, inter alios, a number of celebrities.

See also 'inter alia'.

in toto

This means 'totally' or 'entirely'. This example is from a newspaper article:

Indeed, sometimes a colleague would write a letter in toto, and Einstein would simply add his signature at the end.

intra vires

This means 'within the powers' and is used to describe lawful actions that an individual or institution takes. For example:

The government acted intra vires when it passed the legislation.

See also 'ultra vires'.

ipso facto

This means 'by that very fact' and is used to mean 'irrespective of any other factors, including considerations of right and wrong'. For example:

Despite the extreme circumstances of the case, he is ipso facto guilty of murder.

magnum opus

This means 'a great work' and is used to describe someone's greatest work. For example:

Middlemarch *is George Eliot's magnum opus.*

mala fide

This means 'in bad faith' and is the opposite of 'bona fide'. See also 'bona fide'.

mea culpa

This means 'by my fault' and is used to say, 'I am to blame'. For example:

"Mea culpa," he said. "I left the door open and now the cat's missing."

memento mori

This means 'remember to die' and is used to refer to an object, for example, a skull, that reminds us we will inevitably die.

modus operandi

This means 'method of working'. When the police refer to a criminal's 'M.O.' they are talking about his 'modus operandi': the way he goes about committing a crime. However, the term can be applied to any activity. See also 'modus vivendi'.

modus vivendi

This means 'a way of living' and is used to describe a compromise or accommodation that a group of people come to when they have to get along together. For example:

The scientists, cooped up together in the spacecraft for three months, would have to reach a modus vivendi.

See also 'modus operandi'.

ne plus ultra

This means 'not more beyond' and is used to describe 'the best there is' or 'the highest possible achievement'. For example:

Middlemarch *is the ne plus ultra of George Eliot's work.*

nil desperandum

This means 'nothing is to be despaired of' and is commonly used to mean 'never say die' or 'don't give up' or 'don't despair'.

NB

This is an abbreviation of 'nota bene', meaning 'note well'.

non sequitur

This means 'it does not follow' and is used to highlight the fact that one thing does not logically follow on from another. The following is an example of a non sequitur:

You're very rich and so must be very happy.

op. cit. (scholarly)

This is short for 'opere citato' and means 'in the work cited'. It is usually used in an author's notes or footnotes as a brief way of telling the reader that the full name of the publication being referred to has already been cited.

passim (scholarly)

This means 'here and there' and is used to tell the reader that a topic just mentioned is also discussed in a variety of other places within the publication or series of publications.

pax

This means 'peace'.

per diem

This means 'by the day'. It can be used to mean 'daily' or 'every day' and can also mean a payment to cover daily expenses.

per se

This means 'by or in itself'. It is used to mean 'intrinsically'. For example:

I don't dislike red per se, I just don't think it suits me.

persona grata

This means 'an acceptable person'. Its opposite is 'persona non grata' as in, 'he is persona non grata' (*not* 'he is *a* persona non grata').

pp

This stands for 'per procurationem' or in its shortened form, 'per pro'. It means 'by delegation to'. The abbreviation 'pp' (always written lower case) is used at the end of a letter when someone signs on behalf of someone else. (Sometimes people get it the wrong way round.) If Bill Smith is signing on behalf of Sarah Green, this should be written:

Sarah Green pp Bill Smith

… and not the other way round.

prima facie

This means 'at first sight' and is a legal term, as in 'prima facie evidence', meaning there are sufficient facts and evidence to suggest someone's guilt unless this can be disproved. For example:

We have prima facie evidence: he was found holding the smoking gun.

primus inter pares

This means 'the first among equals'. Strictly speaking, it refers to a man. The equivalent term for a woman is 'prima inter pares'. The term is most commonly used in relation to the prime minister of Great Britain. For example:

He is primus inter pares.

pro bono

This fairly well-known phrase is a shortened version of 'pro bono publico' meaning 'for the public good'. It is a phrase very often used when describing work carried out by lawyers for free. For example:

The barrister took on the work pro bono.

pro rata

This means 'in proportion'. Most people are familiar with this term thanks to job advertisements for part-time positions which offer 'pro-rata' salaries; in other words, a proportion of the full-time salary.

pro tempore

This means 'temporarily' and is often abbreviated to 'pro tem'. For example, a 'leader pro tem' will stay in office until someone permanent is appointed.

quid pro quo

This means 'something for something'. For example:

We will give them an extra day off as a quid pro quo for working at the weekend.

QED

This is short for 'quod erat demonstrandum' and means 'which was to be demonstrated'. It is most appropriately used at the end of a mathematical solution to claim that the problem has been solved.

Q.V. (scholarly)

This is an abbreviation of 'quod vide' meaning 'which see'. It is used to tell the reader that an explanation for what has been written (perhaps a particularly obscure term or unusual word) is provided elsewhere in the publication.

reductio ad absurdum

This means 'reduction to absurdity' and is used to describe an argument or proposition that leads to an absurd or illogical conclusion. This example of its use is from a newspaper article:

A standard Whitehall technique when confronted by embarrassing allegations is to dismiss them by caricature or resorting to a kind of reductio ad absurdum.

sic (scholarly)

This means 'thus'. This word is written in brackets after an unusual or unexpected word to assure the reader that it is not a typo. For example:

Mr Smyth (sic) joined the meeting after lunch.

sine die

This means 'without a day' and is used to mean 'no day has been fixed'. So if your favourite film has been withdrawn from the cinema sine die, go out and buy the DVD unless you're prepared to wait indefinitely for its return.

sine qua non

This means 'without which not'. It is used to mean 'an indispensable requirement'. For example:

The re-election of the chairwoman is a sine qua non for the continued success of the committee.

stet (scholarly)

This means 'let it stand'. The word is used by proofreaders when they initially cross out a word or section of text, but then change their mind and decide to keep it in. They highlight the text they want to keep by underlining it with a broken line and adding the word 'stet' next to it.

sub judice

This means 'before the courts'. You will often hear people in public life say:

I can't discuss this particular case as it's sub judice.

It means the matter is still being dealt with by the law and should not be discussed in public by anyone involved in the case.

sui generis

This means 'of its own kind' and is used to mean 'unique'. For example:

The film is a sui generis masterpiece.

supra (scholarly)

This is a term used by writers to draw the reader's attention to something written earlier in the publication. See also 'vide supra' and 'vide infra'.

tabula rasa

This means 'a scraped writing tablet' and is used to describe a 'clean slate', as when someone approaches an activity with fresh eyes and without preconceptions.

tempus fugit

This means 'time flies'.

terra firma

This means 'solid land'. For example:

I was glad to be back on terra firma after the long flight.

terra incognita

This means 'unknown territory' and is used to describe places or subject areas which are unknown. For example:

Pure mathematics is terra incognita to me.

Having crossed the border, we found ourselves in terra incognita.

ultra vires

This means 'beyond the powers' and is used to describe actions taken by individuals or institutions that are outside their legal powers. For example:

The council acted ultra vires when it ordered the building to be demolished.

See also 'intra vires'.

ut infra (scholarly)

This means 'as below' or 'as cited below'.

ut supra (scholarly)

This means 'as above', or 'as cited above'.

veni, vidi, vici

This means 'I came, I saw, I conquered'.

vice versa

This means 'the other way round' or 'conversely' and is a common expression in English.

vide infra (scholarly)

This means 'see below'. A writer can use this phrase to draw the reader's attention to something written later in the publication. See also 'vide supra' and 'supra'.

vide supra (scholarly)

This means 'see above'. A writer can use this phrase to draw the reader's attention to something written earlier in the publication. See also 'supra' and 'vide infra'.

vivat

This means 'long live' as in 'vivat the emperor'.

viz

This is short for 'videlict' meaning 'it is permitted to see'. It is used to mean 'namely' or 'to wit'. For example:

I sold most of my stock, viz all the stationery and most of the office furniture.

vox populi

This means 'the voice of the people' and is much more commonly known as 'vox pop'. For example:

The journalist did a quick vox pop on the streets to find out what people thought.

French words and phrases

aide-mémoire

This is from the French 'aider' meaning 'to help' and 'mémoire' meaning 'memory'. It simply means some form of reminder.

aperçu

This comes from 'apercevoir' meaning to 'perceive' or 'catch sight of'. 'Aperçu' means an insight or an outline.

apropos

This derives from 'à-propos' meaning 'aptness' or 'to the purpose' and is used to describe something that is appropriate. It can also form the phrase 'apropos of' meaning 'in respect of'.

It is also used in the following way to mean that something has been said out of the blue:

He told me his wife had left apropos of nothing.

au courant

This means 'up to date' and is used most often in relation to someone being au courant with current affairs, but can also refer to the latest fashion.

beau geste

This means a fine, noble or gracious act or gesture. The plural is 'beaux gestes'.

beau monde

This phrase describes the world of fashion and high society.

bête noire

This term, meaning 'black beast', is used to refer to something or someone particularly disliked or dreaded. For example:

Sitting exams is my bête noire.

The plural is 'bêtes noires'.

bien pensant

Adjective: conventional or orthodox in attitude.

bien-pensant (note the added hyphen)

Noun: a conventional or orthodox person.

bon mot

This means 'good word' and is used to describe a clever, witty or fitting comment.

bon vivant

This is used to describe someone who enjoys the high life, especially luxurious food and drink. In English, we also use the term 'bon viveur', but this is not used in French. The plural of bon vivant is 'bons vivants'.

carte blanche

When a person or organisation has carte blanche ('blank paper') it means they have unrestricted power or discretion to act as they please. The plural is 'cartes blanches'.

cause célèbre

This phrase is used to refer to a famous trial, legal dispute or controversy. The plural is 'causes célèbres'.

comme ci comme ça

This means 'so-so', 'average' or 'indifferent'. For example:

The standard of food in the hotel was comme ci comme ça.

comme il faut

This phrase is used to mean 'correct' or 'fitting'. For example:

It was comme il faut that he was sacked on the spot.

coup de grâce

In the sense of being a 'blow of mercy' this phrase is used to mean the delivery of a final, fatal blow, very often as an act of mercy. However, the phrase is also used in a more upbeat sense. For example:

Following an astonishing array of tricks, the magician's coup de grâce was to pull a live elephant from her sleeve.

The plural is 'coups de grâce'.

coup d'état

This phrase ('stroke of state') is used to describe a sudden or violent takeover of governmental power. The plural is 'coups d'état'.

cri de coeur

This is a passionate or heartfelt appeal. It is a slight distortion of the French phrase, 'cri du coeur' (cry of the heart). The plural is 'cris de coeur'.

de rigueur

If something is de rigueur ('of strictness') it is required by the rules of etiquette, social norms, or standards of fashion. For example:

It is de rigueur to stand when she comes into the room.

Black hats and matching shoes are de rigueur this season.

de trop

This describes something that is too much, unwanted or in the way. In French, it literally means 'of too much'. This example is from the *Guardian* newspaper:

But should a trip to America for some decent shirts seem a little de trop, there is succour in this country.

en famille

This can be used to describe being at home with one's family, or doing things in an informal and friendly way.

enfant terrible

An enfant terrible ('terrible child') is a person much given to making outrageous or outspoken remarks, or behaving in an unconventional way. For example:

He is the enfant terrible of the arts world.

The plural is 'enfants terribles'.

entre nous

When speaking 'entre nous', we are speaking confidentially or just between ourselves. For example:

I must tell you, entre nous, that I am applying for another job.

fait accompli

If something is a fait accompli, it is irreversible or beyond alteration (an 'accomplished fact'). For example:

The marriage is a fait accompli.

The plural is 'faits accomplis'.

faux pas

If you commit a faux pas ('false step') you have made a social blunder. The plural of faux pas is the same as the singular (one faux pas or two faux pas).

je ne sais quoi

This means 'I know not what'. If someone or something has a certain je ne sais quoi, they have an elusive and usually very attractive quality that is hard to define.

mise en scène

This phrase is used to describe the setting for a stage play, or the objects used in such a setting. It can also mean, more generally, the setting or environment where an event takes place.

mot juste

The mot juste is the exact or most appropriate word or expression for the particular circumstances. The plural is 'mots justes'.

nom de guerre

This means 'war name' and is used to mean 'pseudonym'. The plural is 'noms de guerre'.

nom de plume

This simply means 'pen name'. The plural is 'noms de plume'.

savoir-faire

Savoir-faire means knowing how to do and say things correctly. For example:

She demonstrated great savoir-faire when dealing with the foreign visitors.

tout de suite

This means 'at once' or 'straightaway'.

tout le monde

This phrase is used to mean 'everyone' or 'all the world'.

Other foreign words and phrases

aficionado

This word, derived from Spanish, means an ardent fan, devotee or supporter. The plural is 'aficionados'.

angst

From the German, this word means 'acute dread and anxiety'. For example:

The thought of speaking in public caused him angst.

dolce vita

An Italian phrase meaning 'the sweet life' or 'the good life', often associated with physical pleasure.

doppelgänger

This German word literally means 'double-goer' and is used in English to mean an exact ghostly double of someone. (Don't confuse this with the Doppler effect which is to do with changes in sound or light wave frequency.)

glasnost

This Russian word means 'publicity' or 'openness'. It became common currency in the 1980s under the leadership of Mikhail Gorbachov in the former Soviet Union when he introduced a policy of public openness and accountability. See also 'perestroika'.

hoi polloi

This Greek phrase literally means 'the many' and is used to refer to the 'common' people. Sometimes, people mistakenly use this phrase to refer to 'posh' people.

perestroika

This Russian word means 'reconstruction' and was commonly used in the UK media in the 1980s to refer to Mikhail Gorbachov's efforts to reconstruct the economy of the former Soviet Union. See also 'glasnost'.

schadenfreude

The English language has borrowed this word from the German to mean 'taking pleasure in someone else's misfortune'. For example:

The schadenfreude he felt when his friend was demoted filled him with shame.

sotto voce

From the Italian meaning 'under one's voice', this means to speak quietly or in an undertone to avoid being overheard.

Zeitgeist

This German word, literally meaning 'time spirit', is used to describe the spirit, outlook or attitude of a particular time or place. For example:

The prevailing zeitgeist meant people rarely dared to protest.

Foreign Words and Phrases: Index

Latin words and phrases 127
ab initio 127
ad hoc 127
ad hominem 128
ad infinitum 128
a fortiori 128
ad nauseam 128
alumna/alumnus/alumni 129
annus mirabilis 129
annus horribilis 129
ante bellum 129
bona fide 130
bona fides 130
carpe diem 130
casus belli 130
caveat emptor 130
circa 131
cogito ergo sum 131
compos mentis 131
cui bono? 131
cum laude 131
de facto 132
de jure 132
de profundis 132
deus ex machina 132
emeritus/emerita 133
erratum 133
ergo 133
et al (1) 133
et al (2) 133
et tu, Brute? 134
ex cathedra 134

exempli gratia 134
ex gratia 134
habeas corpus 135
ibid 135
id est 135
in flagrante delicto 135
infra dig 135
in loco parentis 136
in medias res 136
inter alia 136
inter alios 136
in toto 137
intra vires 137
ipso facto 137
magnum opus 137
mala fide 138
mea culpa 138
memento mori 138
modus operandi 138
modus vivendi 138
ne plus ultra 139
nil desperandum 139
NB 139
non sequitur 139
op. cit. 140
passim 140
pax 140
per diem 140
per se 140
persona grata 141
pp 141
prima facie 141
primus inter pares 141
pro bono 142

pro rata...142
pro tempore 142
quid pro quo...142
QED..143
Q.V..143
reductio ad absurdum 143
sic...143
sine die 144
sine qua non 144
stet 144
sub judice...144
sui generis 145
supra...145
tabula rasa..145
tempus fugit...145
terra firma..145
terra incognita..146
ultra vires 146
ut infra...146
ut supra 146
veni, vidi, vici 146
vice versa 147
vide infra (scholarly)...147
vide supra 147
vivat...147
viz 147
vox populi...147
French words and phrases 148
aide-mémoire 148
aperçu...148
apropos 148
au courant...149
beau geste 149
beau monde..149

bête noire	149
bien pensant	149
bien-pensant	149
bon mot	150
bon vivant	150
carte blanche	150
cause célèbre	150
comme ci comme ça	150
comme il faut	151
coup de grâce	151
coup d'état	151
cri de coeur	151
de rigueur	152
de trop	152
en famille	152
enfant terrible	152
entre nous	153
fait accompli	153
faux pas	153
je ne sais quoi	153
mise en scène	153
mot juste	154
nom de guerre	154
nom de plume	154
savoir-faire	154
tout de suite	154
tout le monde	155
Other foreign words and phrases	155
aficionado	155
angst	155
dolce vita	155
doppelgänger	155
glasnost	156
hoi polloi	156

perestroika 156
schadenfreude 156
sotto voce 157
Zeitgeist 157

Notes

About the Author

Deborah is a qualified journalist and professional copywriter.

This book grew from her successful blog, also called Wordwatch.

In 2013, Deborah set up Bennison Books to publish outstanding undiscovered authors, favourite and forgotten classics, and useful non-fiction works (including this one!).

Bennison Books also publishes poetry under its Poetic Licence imprint.

Bennison Books

Bennison Books has four imprints:

Contemporary Classics
Great writing from new authors

Non-Fiction
Interesting and useful works written by experts

People's Classics
Handpicked golden oldies by favourite and forgotten authors

Poetic Licence
Poetry and prosetry

Bennison Books is named after Ronald Bennison,
an aptly named blessing.

Follow Bennison Books on Twitter
twitter.com/BennisonBooks
Join Bennison Books on Facebook
facebook.com/BennisonBooks
Bennison Books
bennisonbooks.wordpress.com

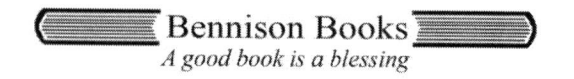

Bennison Books
A good book is a blessing